THE SYLVIA HOTEL POEMS

THE SYLVIA HOTEL POEMS

George Fetherling

George Fetherling

QUATTRO BOOKS

The publication of *The Sylvia Hotel Poems* has been generously supported by the Canada Council for the Arts.

Canada Council   Conseil des Arts
for the Arts   du Canada

Cover photograph: George Fetherling
Author's photograph: Merrill Fearon
Cover design: Diane Mascherin

Library and Archives Canada Cataloguing in Publication

Fetherling, George
  The Sylvia Hotel poems / George Fetherling.

ISBN 978-0-9810186-9-0

1. Poetry, Canadian (English)--British Columbia--Vancouver. I. Title.

PS8561.E834S94 2010   C811'.54   C2010-900330-6

Published by Quattro Books
P.O. Box 53031, Royal Orchard Postal Station
10 Royal Orchard Blvd., Thornhill, ON L3T 3C0
www.quattrobooks.ca

Printed in Canada

Also by George Fetherling

Poetry

Rites of Alienation
The Dreams of Ancient People
Selected Poems
Madagascar: Poems & Translations
Singer, An Elegy

Fiction

The File on Arthur Moss
Jericho
Tales of Two Cities: A Novella Plus Stories
Walt Whitman's Secret

Travel

Running Away to Sea
Three Pagodas Pass
One Russia Two Chinas

Memoir

Travels by Night

Contents

I meet a better class of people in my dreams.

—Paul Goodman (1911-72)

Foreword

Most of these poems were written as though in obedience to W.H. Auden's somewhat unexpected dictum that the person who stops writing love poems has stopped writing poetry altogether. Here the specific subject is unrequited love. Four hundred years' worth of Italian opera has taught us that the role of the unrequited lover is not an easy one. But surely the beginning of mature (post-operatic) wisdom, it seems to me, is understanding that the life of the unrequiting lovee is no walk in Stanley Park either.

As for the title, the Sylvia Hotel is a cherished eight-storey Vancouver landmark that might, in general terms, be compared to the Chelsea in New York or the Chateau Marmont in Hollywood. That is to say, writers, visual artists and musicians, both local and visiting, and indeed many other people working in various cultural trades, have long done their drinking there, or their sleeping, or both. It is located in the West End, which is sometimes called Canada's most densely populated neighbourhood, and is bounded by Gilford Street (where the main entrance is), Pendrell Street and Beach Avenue. The last of these takes its name from English Bay Beach, which is directly opposite the hotel. The beach can be viewed from the big windows in the Sylvia's storied bar, which in 1954 became the first American-style cocktail lounge in Vancouver and which some patrons treat as though it were their office or house of worship.

Like so many the city's most comfortable buildings, the hotel was built in 1912, the year that the great Vancouver real estate bubble was about to burst, as British capital was redirected to other opportunities. Originally it was a bloc of flats called the Sylvia Court Apartments, named for the owner's young daughter, Sylvia Goldstein, who lived until 2002, aged 102 (whereupon the flag on the roof was flown at half staff). In 1936, during the Depression, it was made into an apartment-hotel. Only during the Second World War, when it was a haunt of merchant seamen, was it carved up into more or less standard hotel rooms. There are 120 of them in all, including a few that are actually small suites and the two so-called coffin rooms, which are tiny spaces left over when the floor space was reapportioned. It is an independent family-owned hotel and most certainly not a subscriber to any chain aesthetic. The property has been husbanded carefully. It is proudly old-fashioned, resolutely more economical than most hotels that are larger, and indescribably cosy, in a bohemian sort of way. Its policy of accepting dogs as guests probably helps account for the patronage of numerous middle-class English couples of mature years. They coexist uneasily with the artists and journalists who cause them to wander about looking slightly perplexed.

I am one of the great many people who are attracted to the old place. It sometimes seems to me that a majority of the turning points in my life have somehow been connected to the Sylvia. After all these years, this pattern of coincidence is becoming just a trifle spooky.

GEOGRAPHER

I would be a geographer
if I were your lover
bathing you with a small soapy cloth
charting the archipelago the
vertebrae make
stepping stones down your thin back that
disappear beneath the waterline.
I would name these Le Isole del Desiderio
for the way I hope you might feel
sitting in the iron tub singing
softly to yourself.

Later, that cat whose life we saved
at the market would wake us gently
playing soccer beneath our bed
batting a fig with its tiny paws.

THE SYLVIA

Vines grow thick and knotted
that squirrels might use them
as a staircase to peek into the
rooms of lovers peering out.
They hope for a little food
or failing that a safe glimpse
of how life is pursued
on the other side of the glass.

People told me that I lacked amber
to warn of change or promise it:
a traffic signal with only green and red
with no light to separate joy from impatience.
They were avid for such metaphors
as this.

Now I have real amber mounted
in a silver ring and live at the Sylvia Hotel
where the only way to know the season
is to look out the window and note the
colour of the ivy.

Half the year, the green of
first life. Otherwise the waxy red
of the reborn emotion we hope exists
in case we ever need it.

I CALL TO THE WINDOWS

I call to the windows
to witness the way I decode
the new language of your laughter.
Stand ready to be surprised, I say
almost daring events to unravel.

My thoughts enunciate sharply
what you do not wish to hear.
One day speech will slip out.
It just got away from me somehow, officer,
like a renegade whipsaw.
I understand.
        You understand
that the worst is not over,
the worst has yet to exhaust itself
in the legacy of old desires
kept folded in wallets or hidden in picture frames
deposited with bankers in Amsterdam
who know all about the utility of secrets
and how to work the system for everything it's worth.

Your absence is my only landmark.
With that and a loonie I can get a coffee.
With that, a compass and a wristwatch
I can't possibly get lost.
On the map my dilemma looks like an accident.

So I walk to the rim of the city
(this takes longer than it used to)
and find that the prairie is still there
beneath the need and the sky.
The lights are like confetti when I
look back, the lies like litter
at my feet.

DOG DREAMS

Every night I wait for the absence to return and free the hostages who lie here beside me. I know to be expectant yet I'm always surprised when the call with its eager demands overtakes me this way. I think, 'If I can just survive one more night of need, I'll start to get my strength back.' The truth is otherwise.

Sometimes I welcome the sensation, stretched out on my right side. I am like a dog having a dream. My hands twitch a little as I mimic the act of running towards you. I utter something but the sound is muffled. I bark in pantomime. This way you'll never know what it is I ask for. Maybe that's all for the best.

Room 243, overlooking the car park

LA BELLE DAME

I do this much better when I'm drunk but the feeling's still here in the morning scrutiny. I need to learn what you can't tell. I know your husband parents siblings but nothing of their wife daughter sister. I couldn't write a play about you because I can't isolate the dramatic turning points. I know only blunt arcs and low trajectories how you've kept your heart honest and beliefs clear accepting the hosts' invitation without letting on that you don't wish to be like them not that they're subtle enough to see that perhaps. I comprehend you in a household where decisions always pooled beneath your feet. 'I won't permit myself to be jam.' 'I'll play along but use my compassion in the service of subversion.' We don't speak of matters because I can't you won't and we each suspect that the other already knows. I for my part have many queries about the body under your clothes. As to the inmate inside the bones I've spent years rearranging question fragments. I don't even know your middle name la belle dame avec beaucoup de merci.

HEALING

I was brilliant until I woke up, it was all true until I
wrote it down to suture the wounds that beg for
treatment. In giving them names I've killed what feeds
them. Whatever heals is soon enough forgotten and I
don't want that to happen here. Are you strong enough
to stand it? Of course you are, women don't think about
being brave they just commit bravery without effort. No
one's quite so sure about me.

My language is not improvised it's merely inadequate to
these fits of stylish delirium. The direction I've come
from tells you who I'm not, just one sorry confidant
looking for his sister writing hard to understand the still-
life tragedies but always one tragedy behind: that which
never went away. Feelings have a way of leaking out at
the most inopportune moments. The window is narrow
the love is long.

*Room 429, southeast corner, view
of Davie and Denman streets and
of the small triangular park*

STORYLINE

I was in love with a text long before we met
and there's still a faint aftertaste of narrative

when I pry myself away from your mouth in that dream
I wrote. This is final they say. Work in the hope

of nothing less than entirely new creativities.
We will collaborate without quarrelling

or meaning to be so obvious about
the hidden seriousness beneath our repartee.

We will defend ourselves vigorously
against charges of conspiracy to traffic in art.

The books will fight back. With music and
painting we could bring a class action.

I crave to be embedded in the story of your journey
and watch your face as I worship your advice.

RUSSELL SQUARE

What a sweet bit of history this will be.
How you emerged from the backlog
of people waiting to be born
and grew to dream of creating new freedoms
as I attended the act of making
and we groomed each other like monkeys.

That is how I imagine it might have been.

My heart is no bigger than a dragon fruit
but it has travelled.
Having no photographs of you, I carry these ones
of other women with the faces cut out,
and looking at the ovals of blackness
imagine you, when not caught in sunlight,
in some heavily curtained third-storey room
near Russell Square dancing
with yourself instead of with me
to a wind-up gramophone that plays
only the tunes I write in praise of you.

HANGOVERS AND REGRET

I can't be blamed for failing
to learn the unknowable
neither can you fault me for wishing.
The only reason I drink all this wine
is that it lets me think of you more clearly
you're not the sort of person who puts
up with any nonsense from me or Nature
the power you have is warm but it is
power you do not want over someone
you dare not acknowledge.

I despise the expanse you keep between us
that slowly fills up with the past
like never-ending invisible snowfalls
silent comforting suffocating cold
methodical until they turn lovely
frostbite and exposure result
from hangovers and regret.

I keep watch on your window
so burn a red candle if you agree or
merely understand that we cannot
wash the truth out of ourselves.

THIEF

I write only so that you might at least be conscious that my gift to you is this predicament I have put us in but which only I have been aware of. I want you to know the surroundings. You will wish to destroy this after reading it (I certainly would) but that's no reason to forget. I have always kept most of myself in the middle distance where sharpness and colour aren't so important as in the foreground where you reside, for that is where you have preferred me to be. There are facts you don't possess, need or desire.

I was raised in a cave and home-schooled—cave-schooled —growing in the darkness like a mushroom ignorant of his brother mushrooms, as unfamiliar with the world beyond as a giant tortoise that would suppose, if capable of considering the point, that the rest of the world must be the same as his own Galapagos boondocks. I grew and went old in isolation like one of those Japanese soldiers who used to turn up from time to time on obscure Pacific atolls not realising that the Second World War had ended, and had done so in someone else's favour, emerging awkward and a bit eccentric, an item in the cabinet of curiosities that the news already had become... 'I am your two-headed calf' I started to say. 'Here, I'm sorry, but tact must intervene' you say—tactfully.

I'm uncomfortable using the personal pronoun but what am I to do? The story of the circumstance is freed now from his long incarceration between the lines. I write mainly to explain how I learned virtually nothing at the time but am grateful that I so often appeared, all too briefly and at the last possible historical moment, to become a witness—again, without understanding the events as they occurred.

I was there when you were so beautiful to everyone and not just to me. I saw you stride in confident compassion on long legs with shoulders drawn back, straight of spine, the chest cavity open full wide, your hair your breasts your eyes ripe with the wisest love. You were always the smartest person in the room and the kindest. I waited on the act of your being and am privileged therefore. I stand among these trees and slowly become one of them, part of the arbutus diaspora. I am proud of what little friendship I've been able to steal. Yes I am the Good Thief, skilled but somehow benign. You may know me yet and hear me when I play on the black keys exclusively. You will recognise me: I'll be wearing the soutane I bought for the ceremony.

EURIPIDES

Euripides was praised for his fresh take on tragedy
or rather the retailing of it
for nothing really changes in the silent commission
or at least always changes in precisely the same way.
As the poet (Ko Un of Korea) says:
Forever does the boat travel from you to me
and back again but the boat of no return
can only depart.

Please tell the audience this when you learn of it:
how with nothing lost to the open air
that is the price of constant mindful observance
I was fortunate to love you in my heart
in restaurants and on public transit and in mind
and die with all my faults intact, retreating under cover
of insincere approval delivered to the wrong address.

THE VOICE IS THE PUBLIC HEART

The voice is the public heart and yours
is a whisper on the water that seems
to come from different directions
depending on where I stand.
On the beach in the dark I listen for it.
I beckon it and it answers
mocking me with all its healing powers
and the message is always one of justice
and freedom from manufactured terror
such as my own that some night I'll be left
with only the sound of the punctured surf
as it continues to abuse the shore.

The gravitation of confidence pulls the other way now
and what is close to me is also closed to me.
Just because I have so many thoughts of you
doesn't mean I choose them at random from
among the miscellaneous.
Each one arises from an untreated ache
to be a part of not apart from you.
You refuse to discuss this in somewhat the way
veterans dislike being asked
to reminisce about their war.

Nonetheless I flatter myself
that we both understand how you sustain me
while I have nothing to give that you need.

ANIMISM (ILLUSTRATED)

The monotheists are arming themselves again.
They cannot see how identical they are
but rise against one another and one day
will come for those of us who believe
that you can't have too many gods so why
should you wish only one.

In my heart I am your lover as surely
as you are your child's mother, your mother's child
for we are all of us partners of
our lover's other loves.
Our sum is no smaller for being shared
among so many.

Why should there not be a god of long life,
another of health, a third of wisdom, a god
of Tuesday mornings and a god of killer storms?
Why can't one who destroys also create
wearing a slightly different costume?

No one wants to sacrifice a goat to ensure
a bountiful harvest. We are a practical people
who happen to accept as true that which we hope
surrounds us like a cosy mist.

SPY

Sometimes the entanglements find us
where we hide and trap us in these mandatory lies.
Surely I'm not the only one who knows
you're working undercover and understands
what runs beneath those tailored suits
and subtle cosmetic urgencies the others
first demanded then came to expect.
You indulge them in your secrets to win
their confidence. How clever that the mole
in their midst should be the brilliant and
compassionate one.

I see your subversion plainly and it touches me.
I am reassured that the youth we ourselves inherited
has been handed off to those who need it more.
We can concern ourselves with different matters now,
I with you and you with me if you would
permit it. But that's impossible.

I cannot be alone in keeping a running count
of all your anonymous wonders.
Perhaps there are others who pour from
the same empty bottle and thank you for the gift
of this oath. The more I speculate the more
I am certain it is true. The hand is
the heart's amanuensis. The lines that
I struggle with so poorly are older
than China, older than poetry.

You are so far away but I am closer
to understanding the distance
whose importance you insist on denying.
You say you find me a little crazy at times.
This is the infiltrator speaking in an
accent gained through rigorous study.
It doesn't fool someone like me who
enjoys imagining that he is privileged
because you have so many other lovers
none of whom you've ever met.

CONFUSION OF THEMES NOT OF MOTIVES

Poems should be wisdom or be love.
Deficient in one I am overstocked in the other
and it must remain my secret that the inventory will be yours
coming to you someday as a puzzling bequest.

The worst sort of ignorance is the kind that bears my name.
It belongs to a prisoner who's locked out and not in
not knowing any possible answers to the questions
I ache to ask, simple questions, the sort
that work their way up through the membranes
in a lifetime of having breakfast.

I've been in this position before, long ago in childhood
when I looked back on my elders and saw their mistakes
as rehearsals for my own
blunder after blunder reaching for the perfect mess
that now I have finally achieved.

I was young and narrow without you because I was
        without you
and the narrowness survived the youth till your appearing
        cured it.
The middle years were those of anguish and desire.
I thought a great deal about Art Deco as one of the culture's
        finest moments
to which you have remained true so tall sleek streamlined,
elegant in your simplicity of line

acknowledging the machine you rebel against but
    respecting it
as the hunter does the animal he singles out: a private
matter between creatures just like the subject at hand.
Your palette of earth tones should be viewed in full
    sunlight.
You are terra cotta with trim of muted silver.
You are my landmark.

MAPPAMUNDI*

Autumn has come and leaves blow aloft
like kites torn apart by competing winds.
At this distance you can't hear the clouds
colliding but only the rain being blotted
on the pavement. Twigs snap. Bones snap.
So many dead.

With untidy mystical visions of the strangers
who need their rest, summon all the travellers
passing through. Bring them together,
hear the conversations of watchful couples
not like us but grown old together, replying
to either's silence with silence of the two together.

Cracks in the ceiling plaster are the rivers
of your body. In the patterns of the mutilated lino
I find faces, yours and those of saints and
everybody's favourite sacred parent.
People always mock me for reinventing
myself, as though this were more than
a form of reincarnation in which we can
all believe. New formats, old loves. Ripening.

You had an insurmountable head start
when I first saw you descending
outfitted in accomplishment top to toe.
Who am I to be blessed by if not by
the one with little stomach for such stupidity
as catching both a cold and an overdose?
It is good that you reject me to keep me even
or so I have believed once or twice.
At this time of year there is heightened
danger of desire.

* 'A map for contemplation, not for use.'

PDFs

You are the first to admit
that I pay you the compliment of
knowing that we stage the event and
only then locate the language
to describe it without explaining it away.

At least I imagine this is how it would be.
It is the tool I use to reconcile the facts
that make up the plot of dreams
over which I've been given custody.
These are PDF episodes, they cannot be
edited. They are fixed and locked. They
are steadfast as I am, defiant as you are.
I am their custodian and nothing more.

When I saw you last you formed a
perfect tall rectangle standing in the doorway.
I was facing in and you were facing out.
Your spacious heart made the
small room enormous.

EMBRACE

Embrace my want and forgive the promise
never to remind you of my residence
this close to the lip of ecstasy and despair.

I struggled to remain faithful to the pledge
but failed. Know that I'm not concerned
or involved but merely observant and devout
straining to infiltrate your dreams.

I write these simple unfashionable lyrics
of no interest whatever to other poets
so you might see me as a male caryatid
holding up the sky lest it crash and
crush us in an avalanche of blue.

Room 202, not a 'coffin room' but
quite tiny, facing Pendrell Street

LA FEMME INSPIRATRICE

How can I scrub away your fear that such a
one-sided subcutaneous relationship should be
a source of fright?

Certainly not by telling you what I came upon today
in that fifty-year-old art book:

someone with your spirit and fulsome understanding
of how what takes place after the horizon
is determined by a silent geometry of its own.

Physically you do not favour her but how would
I come by details of all your calyxes as I have
only imagined them to be?

Until I saw you in the body of someone no doubt
long dead I understood only your public patches
of skin so much like silk like even finer silt and begged
for any anodyne response.

Such has been the amount of the matter frankly
and through time.

'Won't you stay and have more wine that
I might know your thinking?'
The tactic has never worked and now my files
are a total loss.

I was shortlisted for oblivion until this afternoon
but now I can lust as well as long. This concludes
my application.

Sometimes I feel like a New Yorker cartoon.
A poet goes into a bar and says to the bartender
'My muse doesn't understand me.'

EDO

A gentleman appeared to us
in a dream of ancient Edo.

We knew he was a gentleman
for he carried both swords,
long and short, the daito and the tanto.

We knew it was Edo from the way
that wasps spun houses of paper
that looked so Japanese
showing the simplicity that
only great skill affords.

We knew it was a dream
because he was travelling
at the speed of darkness
or we were.

He came here on an errand of diplomacy.

Now is the time to gather our lessons
and concentrate on what can be accomplished.
The moment to begin fresh obsessions
is at hand, lit only by dusk,
never by sunrise.

The ferns toss nervously this way and that
but primp themselves in the breeze
until the messenger of pleasure
appears at the embassy gate.

He is not admitted but feels compelled
to leave this calling card.
You and I find it the following day
in a pile of dismantled clothes.

THE ZONE

1.

Who can listen in on silent conversations
or return to what never existed?
No one

ever deeds back the past to let
spilt colour colonise the spots that
lie barren.

I have built this hidden tower not
for spying but to honour you
in these disputed border lands.
The story works much like a play
but tells us things only poetry says.

As you pursue your course, I pursue mine
hoping that those you like you also love.

2.

I stumble whenever I move forward.
Every time I return here, the place
seems so much less without you.
Come away with me to some other coast
where there are various forms of plant life
that are local to our mission.
Lateral migration. Birds have the wrong idea.

I will take every care of you. I won't let you
breathe in such a way as to put stress
on your skeletal frame. Or as I prefer
to say: stimulate it.

The process of decay when followed
conscientiously can lead to a slower
confrontation with obscurity or far more rapid recognition.
Take me up as though I were a cause.
Pack a bag and cancel your subscriptions.
Let me teach you something for a change.

TONTINE

A kind person requiring kindness
took an interest in me when
we met on the long highway
heading in opposite directions
towards the caravansaries.
We plotted sagely in a piece
of crazy China set down here.
In living memory there was nothing
quite like what I felt or grew to feel.
But the dead, they forget nothing,
not a favour or a slight,
and one can find them in a glass of
this snake whisky the old men drink
to restore their vigour since it cannot
suppress their desire.

The heart locates a way
but I am the fruit of my ruin.
If I were you and you were me
and you were the first to die
I would revive the ancient art of mourning
for as long as the crocuses continue to appear.

FIRST SIGNS OF WARTIME SPRING

Eleven ships in English Bay this morning
impatient for their turn at the gantries
ten or more every day so far this month
business in China must be good
cherry blossoms underfoot like confetti
once the echoes evaporate
I leave my footprints until the next breeze.

The Americans have a new war
that's how we know the generations have changed
but we're not headlines we don't need verbs
to validate ourselves.
To the east, the shoulder of the sky is hunched
in back of the sun, still arguing for acceptance
begging us to go there.
The strategy is to let the future emerge
a little at a time that we might grow accustomed
and not protest or go mad.
The window opens so briefly that we cannot
throw out the words.
This will have to do for now.

Mountains to the north zoom in
on people currently between destinations
it's time to harvest the lessons
tomorrow is deep yesterday shallow
sometimes the other way round.
Be like the cave-dwelling hermit
who learns from the mute and mocks
the big yellow bruise.
Slideshow over, the screen goes white
we revert to ritual avoidance of rituals
as practised by lordly bureaucrats who seldom
deviate from what they receive.

The meaningless courage of the entourage
fails them as usual.

Dawn dusk inhale exhale
at night when the stars tremble
we will have no comfort to offer
consumed as we are in events we observe
yet refuse to follow.
Old before my time in relation
to the time available
I spend my declining years declining to accept
struggling to continue trusting the voice
that is the public function of the heart.
In the end, succour finds its own level
everyone fingers everybody else
everyone forgives everybody else
we're all subsidiaries of one another
whatever I know I've learned by
eavesdropping.

Vancouver, April 2005

SONG

As the deck of cards comes apart when expertly shuffled
by shifty fingers so does the blossom accelerate then
explode in your face silently once you've bent to embrace
its aroma. The demi-lunes of the cuticles remind you of
sunrise (the right hand) and sunset (the left). You need
no further tattoos in the margins of books for the impact
alone decorates so fiercely, black on white. You stare
across the water at the mountains, the same view that
first opened your eyes to trade. That was before the map
stopped growing.

The perfume bottle was filled with mace. The cornucopia
became an avalanche that spilled out on the thick carpet
of mistakes. What happened next took place outside our
knowledge; being cautious, the necromancers called in
sick and viewed the whole affair with the sort of
reproach common to their kind. Retract its plunger and
the syringe extracts the pain. Those of you who follow
won't be disappointed. You've been here long enough to
see in the dark. But stay too long and you'll glow that
others might find you without effort.

He was a master of what he called the backslash
withdrawal defence. Sure he was a thief but before going
buried bits of treasure for the legacy-hunters to find. He
knew that poetry is something done with the hands, like
pottery or embalming, and that sometimes dirt gets
under the nails. Gloves are for cowards who don't love
truth. If he were here now I'd say these things and more.
I'd say: We all need secrets that can't get out and the god
who loves the extrovert also loves the lurker. I'd say: This
is a song to you.

TWENTY-ONE HAIKU FROM THE SYLVIA HOTEL BAR (FOR SUSAN MICHELACCI)

Betting that a hunch will strike
small groups of foreigners
sitting round a fire

Snow pack heavy in the mountains this year
death lacks only an opening line
time to update the résumé

Sun goes down laser straight
little hope of rescue
file an incident report

Clouds crash into one another
at this distance pantomime is all we get
somebody stole the remote again

Chainsaw sounds coming from the vacuum!
hotel terror! negligent grace!
the luxury of distraction!

The moon was shining all over us
lucky drunken daylight
feasts while others fast

Champagne and Chinese food
the drip becomes a spectacle
helicopters nervous but not us

Around obstacles where possible
over them when necessary
water trying its best to be quiet

Now where? nowhere
apocalypse on both your houses
distant fairgrounds

Aperçus await recycling
metaphor whores linger at the entrance
garbage strike now five weeks long

Change for the changeless
help make the homeless homeful again
swap spare motif for a little bit of process?

Only five percent of collections on exhibit
the good stuff kept in the dungeons
beneath the dance floor

Memory triggers comfort
still hum the tune her phone number played
police station coffee on a frosty morning

This is the room all right
cured within the privacy of the moment
you were in fine voice that evening

Up streets and alleys in between
moving like participles
cavity scarcity scar city

Drained of words at end of day
everybody wants more sentences
the unexpurgated life is not worth living

Yesterday's chaos granted an extension
cherry blossoms return to Nelson Street
so concludes my weekly report

Alleys are valleys between streets
rivers flowing backwards from the sea
disappear as mountain trickles

Leaving me to imagine what spaces contain
reveal just enough to keep yourself safe
has the bamboo taught you nothing?

Years of prep work for these few seconds
no exceptions to universal truths
failure keeps us young

Noon at midnight
lying there in pachinko parlours
harsh light makes shadows for the dead

I ONCE SAW THE MASTER'S SCROLL

I once saw the master's scroll
hovering overhead yet
still enough for me to read
before the characters returned to
themselves becoming a piece
of the hereditary present
with only a smudge of carbon
left behind in the air.

The story it told was frightening.
The narrator rehearsed his finale only once
and hearing the reaction fell silent then rose up,
skinned it, bought it, broke it, missed it.
Where he fitted into the standard
hero cycle I'm not certain.
These things aren't decided in one lifetime.

People like us never go forward
except when eluding capture.
Frost makes a roadbed of the stream
reducing danger, increasing speed.
This is the day to barter for fresh transport
and swap this region for another.

Like you I have a truant disposition.

NAVIGATING CHINATOWN
for A.F. Moritz

Kamikaze snows dive to their death once street lamps
lure them with fraudulent hopes. Visibility so poor,
collars turned up so high, toques pulled down so low that
I barely make out your silhouette tromping along beside
me up Spadina to wherever it may lead us. We try not to
think about destinations but cannot help ourselves,
nostalgic as we are for the time when there was more life
left. The grievous cold and injured dark assign us roles.
Navigating Chinatown.

Thanks to this process called mortality we retain little of
what we were yet remain as much strangers to each other
as once we were only to ourselves. Separating etiquette
from survival has never been difficult for people like us.
To ask someone what name he used in the old country
was rude at best and probably dangerous. Questions were
the leading cause of death in males sixteen to seventy-
five. Our understanding of these courtesies has helped us
persist as safely as we have thus far. It has also diminished
us to the size we are this evening.

Trying to sort out what things to forget before both of us
buckle like two bad knees. We're not here to rush but
there's time enough only for candour. Were you ever in
the business of getting passports for deserters? No, that
was somebody else, I remember now. Spadina isn't Jewish
any more. On a distant day it won't be Chinese either.
But it will still be Spadina full of people who never knew
anyone who remembered somebody who once saw us
when we were alive. The home of farflung afterthoughts
bids you welcome.

POSTDATED

Facing the nightmare
of another winter encampment
starving within sight of the enemy's fires,
late-modern armies often surrendered
in October, the month when death-notices
fill so many columns in the morning papers.

We must not concede just yet
merely from being so worn down
but carefully slowly grow the letters.
However little time remains
still we mustn't hurry: last words
should be words made to last.

'I'm leaving town until this mess
blows over.'

MONET'S FAVOURITE FOG

Monet's favourite fog
was not as so thick as mine.

Sun cold, moon warm
winter's push to summer's pull.

The sun worked hard to rise
this morning but the rain kept
asking to come in.

Usually it's night, always the rain
striking the pavement, sounding
like someone else's applause.

LISTENING POSTS

Exercise one:

Quickly now before it becomes fashionable, monitor the metropolitans. Strain to hear them in Toronto from some unmarked Hamilton address. One that not even the neighbours suspect. This way you pick up slips, chance remarks, badinage, pieces of candour lurking behind all the official pronouncements. No special skills are required.

Exercise two:

Repeat the above substituting Halifax overheard from Dartmouth, San Francisco from Oakland, New Orleans from Algiers. You get the picture. The theory travels well. Portable frontiers.

The theory:

By bridge or ferry across a river or along a short highway a discreet distance removed but not too discreet. Tactful. Listening posts make good neighbours.

The author:

He is sitting on this barstool in downtown Babylon trying hard to remember what he knew back in Zion. The tiny splendours both baffle and console.

ITALIC RAIN

1.

How I might fit in if at all would be
by remaining unfixed, playing the internal

irritant always en route to the next location
comparing each footstep to the last

spilling wine on a page of manuscript.

2.

This evening when I go for a walk alone
the lights across the water are mirrored in such a way

that Kitsilano perches on multicoloured pylons

—revellers howl!

3.

I always place you in the foreground,
you still take long steps backwards

stealing the occasional glance overhead
as though admiring the lights or watching

for the worst sort of predators
keeping yourself safe and your feelings

intact, leaving me to imagine
what the spaces contain.

4.

The night began the day before,
tomorrow is the default.

In the interim, italic rain
and the surprises we need that
can't be set free.

You are my greatest secret.
I don't know what yours is.

SLEEPERS

A sewer polluted by butterflies, the gutters fill and ignite
a fat directory of models and heroes. In mythology there
was a divine being who resolved all one's problems over
lunch, assuming human form, belonging to no group. We
were all polytheists then. But gods sense trouble and
back away.

What hope for however much future remains in messy
times like these when a supplicant must keep moving to
outpace bedlam abandoned on the trail by previous
survivors like so many forged identities, random discards,
no landmarks no arrivals either, vultures loitering on the
horizon?

Available evidence suggests that all the most dangerous
emotions are relentlessly longlived. One stands a better
chance craving the right moment to replace one
impression with another, like a cat burglar inside the
darkened museum. In the end, little that is stolen ever
gets returned, little that is broken repaired. Sometimes
memories on both sides grow weaker that's all.

Those who are most patient inherit what they desire. Or
else lacking recent contact with the Outside, grow too
tired of long delays and live themselves to death. So
much waiting before pouncing makes being a sleeper
slow careful work. Only a few have our talent for it.

THE OTHER PERSON

Sometimes the other person dies first & the next of kin
concedes the matter on behalf of the estate but this isn't
victory by default. Neither party wins, the silence of
those who can't hear is more than strategic quiet. In
certain systems of belief, yesterday's conversation carried
over through today then made permanent is said to be
where the concept of hell originated.

Walk through the past carefully like those homeowners
on the news picking through the rubble of their homes
cursing caprice and fickleness fixing on one or two sad
objects whose loss they wouldn't have noticed if not for
the one big sudden disappearance. Phone calls that
couldn't travel in either direction measured from the
middle.

SPRING RECURS

Spring arrives like a new product with
a major ad campaign behind it.

Look up at the flock of birds.

Their wings don't seem to move.

The bombing commences.

Acknowledgements

'Geographer' first appeared in *The Literary Review of Canada*.

'The Sylvia' prompted a helpful letter from a 'certified arborist' pointing out that the 'ivy' referred to is not in fact ivy, which is evergreen, but rather *Parthenocissus tricuspidata*—which is nevertheless called 'Boston ivy' by lay people. The poem was published in George McWhirter's anthology *A Verse Map of Vancouver* (Anvil Press, 2009).

'I Call to the Windows' was included in *Rocksalt: An Anthology of Contemporary BC Poetry* (Mother Tongue Publishing, 2008), edited by Mona Fertig and Harold Rhenisch.

'Dog Dreams' was in *The Literary Review of Canada*.

The first line of 'Confusion of Themes Not of Motives' is taken from a poem by Robin Skelton from his posthumous collection *In This Poem I Am*, edited by Harold Rhenisch.

'Night Rain' appeared in *Exile*.

'PDFs' was handset and printed letterpress by Nicola Taylor and Neal Maher at Paperbag Press in an edition of 125 copies at Christmas 2007.

'First Signs of Wartime Spring' has appeared in *71(+) for GB: An Anthology for George Bowering*, edited by Jean Baird, David W. McFadden, and George Stanley (privately printed, 2005); *George Fetherling and His Work*, edited by Linda Rogers (Tightrope Books, 2005); and *Crossing Lines*, edited by Allan Briesmaster and Steven Michael Berzensky (Seraphim Editions, 2008).

'Song' appeared in *Exile*.